W9-CCN-491

WOMEN SPORTS STARS

Simone Manuel
Swimming Star

by Heather E. Schwartz

CAPSTONE PRESS
a capstone imprint

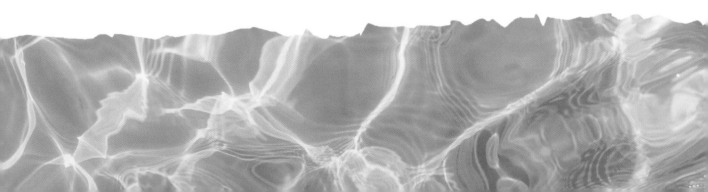

Snap Books are published by Capstone Press,
1710 Roe Crest Drive, North Mankato, Minnesota 56003
www.mycapstone.com

**Cataloging-in-Publication Data is available from the Library of Congress
website.**
ISBN: 978-1-5157-9707-4 (library binding)
ISBN: 978-1-5157-9711-1 (paperback)
ISBN: 978-1-5157-9715-9 (eBook PDF)

Editorial Credits
Abby Colich, editor; Kayla Rossow, designer; Eric Gohl, media researcher;
Katy LaVigne, production specialist

Photo Credits
AP Photo: Darron Cummings, 19, Mark J. Terrill, 17, Matt Patterson, 27; Getty
Images: Adam Pretty, 11, Stringer/Ian MacNicol, 9; Newscom: ABA, 29,
ABACA/Szwarc Henri, 5, AFLO/Yohei Osada, cover, Icon Sportswire/Leslie
Plaza Johnson, 25, Reuters/Athit Perawongmetha, 21, Reuters/Lucy Nicholson,
7, USA Today Sports/Erich Schlegel, 14, USA Today Sports/Robert Stanton, 13;
Shutterstock: Art Alex, 24, Leonard Zhukovsky, 3, 23, LittleWhale, 10, Mario
Savoia, cover (background)

Design Elements: Shutterstock

Printed and bound in the USA.
010780S18

Table of Contents

CHAPTER 1

Making History

The crowd roared with excitement. It was the 2016 Olympic women's 100-meter freestyle. Just 52.70 seconds after it began, the race was over. At the edge of the pool, American swimmer Simone Manuel lifted her goggles. She put her hand to her face in shock. She kissed her finger and raised her hand to the sky. Then she reached over to hug Australian swimmer Cate Campbell in the next lane. Simone started to cry. She swam over to hug Canadian swimmer Penny Oleksiak next.

It was her first Olympics. Simone had just tied for gold. And she'd made history. She was the first female African American swimmer to win Olympic gold in an individual event. Simone was overcome with emotion. With tears in her eyes, she could barely speak to reporters afterward. She told them she felt so blessed.

Simone celebrates her win with Penny Oleksiak during the 2016 Olympics.

FACT

Simone made history in another way too.
Her time of 52.70 was an Olympic record.

CHAPTER 2

Born to Swim

Simone was born August 2, 1996, in Sugar Land, Texas. She started swimming at age 4. Her parents, Sharron and Marc, wanted her to learn so she'd be safe in the water. Simone had also watched her two older brothers compete in swim meets. She wanted to do that too.

Simone's parents thought that after a year of swim lessons, she could join the swim team. On the second day of lessons, however, Simone surprised her mom. She swam across the pool! Simone clearly had a talent for the sport. Soon Simone was swimming with a recreational league. Then she joined Sienna Plantation Aquatics, a competitive swim team.

At age 9 Simone thought about giving up swimming. She wanted to do dance instead. Simone's mom convinced her to try ballet but to keep swimming too. Simone took dance until age 11. Then she gave it up. She was ready to focus just on swimming.

> The first step to competing at a high level is to love the sport you compete in. If you love the sport you choose, you will reach your full potential because you enjoy it.
>
> —Simone Manuel, *Sugar Land Magazine,* Spring 2014

FACT

One reason Simone chose swimming over other sports is because she hates sweating!

Building Swim Skills

By age 11 Simone was swimming on Houston's elite, competitive First Colony Swim Team. Her coach was Allison Beebe. She worked with Simone six days a week. Together they improved Simone's skills in the water. Training was intense, but Allison was careful with the young athlete. She didn't want Simone to burn out.

With two athletic older brothers, Simone wanted to prove herself as an athlete too. Her brothers went on to play college basketball. Simone kept swimming. One of her favorite victories in the pool came when she was 12. She had competed at the same meet the year before. She wasn't happy with her performance. This time around, she did much better. She even broke two State of Texas records.

THE ROLE OF RACE

When she was 11, Simone noticed something. Other swimmers didn't look like her. There were no other African Americans at her swim meets. She started to understand that she represented her race in the sport. Others would view Simone's success as a swimmer as a victory for all African Americans.

Simone during a training swim before a meet

Showing Her Speed

Simone continued to show her talent. At the FINA World Junior Championships in 2011, Simone competed internationally for the first time. She placed fourth in the 100-meter freestyle. The next year she won the 100-meter race at the Junior Pan Pacific Swimming Championships. In 2013 she set a record for her age group in the 50-meter freestyle at the World Championships.

The day after her 17th birthday, Simone competed in the World Championships. In a preliminary race, she swam the 50-meter freestyle in 24.93 seconds. It was the fastest time ever for her age group. It was also the second-fastest time for any American swimmer in history.

Simone in 2013

CHAPTER 3

Olympic Dreams

Simone started college at Stanford University in 2014. As a freshman on the swim team, she won the 50- and 100-yard freestyle individual events at the NCAA Championships. She also won the 400 medley and 400 freestyle relays.

Simone had a packed schedule. She was busy with swimming and her schoolwork. The Olympic trials were at the end of June 2016. If Simone wanted to make the team, the trials would have to be her only focus.

Simone had to make some changes. During her sophomore year, she redshirted from the swim team. She also took time off from her studies.

FACT

Redshirting meant Simone could train with the Stanford team and coach. She just couldn't compete in meets with them. College athletes who redshirt often stay in school an extra year while making up the year of play they missed.

With all her attention on the trials, Simone continued training with her Stanford swim coach. She worked to improve her speed on long course lengths. She competed in non-college meets too. The meets let her see where she stood in her events. Early in June she wasn't too happy with her times. But she knew race strategy mattered more. She was confident her training and practice would pay off.

Simone dives into the pool at a meet in 2015.

STUDIOUS SWIMMER

As a student, Simone cared as much about her studies as she did about swimming. She kept up a 4.0 grade point average in high school. She chose Stanford because she wanted to be challenged in the classroom as well as in the pool.

Trying for the Team

At the trials Simone competed in two events. Only the swimmers who came in first and second in each event would make the 2016 Olympic team.

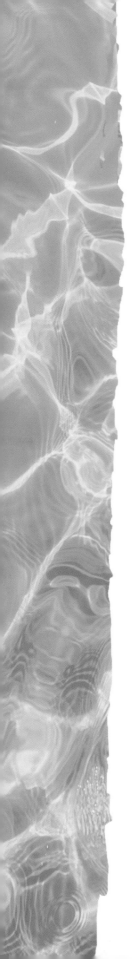

Simone swam the 50-meter freestyle first. Swimmer Abbey Weitziel quickly took the lead. Simone followed close behind. Another swimmer, Madison Kennedy, fought for second. Simone swam fast and stayed strong. By just 0.15 of a second, Simone took second place.

Simone swam in the 100-meter freestyle next. Abbey took the lead again. Swimmer Amanda Weir challenged Simone for second. Again, Simone showed her strength and speed. She touched the wall 0.23 of a second ahead of Amanda. Simone again came in second place. She had made the team! She would be swimming in the Olympics in Rio de Janeiro, Brazil.

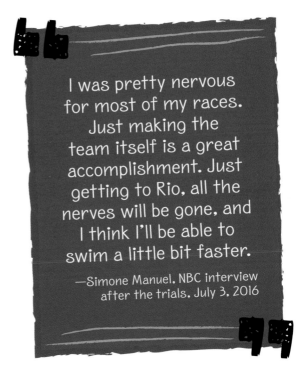

I was pretty nervous for most of my races. Just making the team itself is a great accomplishment. Just getting to Rio, all the nerves will be gone, and I think I'll be able to swim a little bit faster.

—Simone Manuel, NBC interview after the trials, July 3, 2016

It was a life-changing moment for 19-year-old Simone. She was happy, excited, and proud. And she was already thinking ahead to the Olympic Games.

CHAPTER 4

Going for Gold

The 2016 U.S. Women's Olympic Swim Team had 22 members. Eight of Simone's teammates swam in the 2012 Olympics. Joining a team of superstar swimmers could have been intimidating, but they had true team spirit. The veterans wanted Simone to win big too. They knew preparing for the Games meant getting ready mentally as well as physically.

Simone's teammates helped build her confidence. They reminded her that she knew what to do. She knew how to race. They also told her to have fun at her first Olympics.

Simone listened to their advice. She had her own ways to keep calm under pressure too. She tried to focus her mind on things she could control. She knew to work hard to improve her skills and speed. She wouldn't worry about the rest.

My meet day prep is pretty casual. I like to keep things light-hearted and fun. For the most part I'm joking around with my teammates, sending Snapchats, doing anything but focusing on my race. I think that just helps me not have too many nerves.

—Simone Manuel to sports blog SB Nation, August 12, 2016

The 2016 U.S. Olympic swim team

Hitting the Headlines

One thing Simone could not control was the attention she got from the media. Reporters were fascinated with Simone and her teammate Lia Neal.

Lia was a Stanford student too. She was also African American. It was the first time two black swimmers represented the United States in the Olympics together. They both knew they were making history. But they wished the media would focus more on their skills as athletes and less on the color of their skin.

Questions from reporters and stories in the news sometimes upset Simone and Lia. Because of this, the two teammates bonded and grew closer. They talked about what they were going through and the pressures they felt.

Simone with Lia Neal (right)

FACT

The first black female U.S. Olympic swimmer was Maritza Correia. She earned a silver medal in the 4 x 100-meter medley relay in the 2004 Games.

Racing in Rio

Finally, the Olympic Games began. The 100-meter freestyle was Simone's first event. The buzzer sounded. Simone dove in with a strong start. But the attention was on one of her competitors, Australian swimmer Cate Campbell. A month earlier, Cate had broken the 100 freestyle world record. Cate was the favorite expected to take the gold.

Halfway into the race, Cate edged to the lead. Her sister, Bronte Campbell, followed close behind. It looked as if the sisters could earn both the gold and silver medals. And then there was Simone. She was headed for third place as she raced to the finish.

Suddenly, Simone began to pull ahead of both Campbell sisters. So did Canadian swimmer Penny Oleksiak. Fans screamed louder and louder at the upset they were seeing. Simone and Penny finished the 100-meter freestyle at exactly the same time. They had tied for first place. Simone had earned her first Olympic gold medal. She'd also earned her place in history.

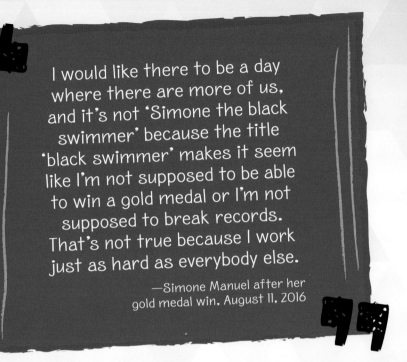

I would like there to be a day where there are more of us, and it's not 'Simone the black swimmer' because the title 'black swimmer' makes it seem like I'm not supposed to be able to win a gold medal or I'm not supposed to break records. That's not true because I work just as hard as everybody else.

—Simone Manuel after her gold medal win, August 11, 2016

Simone and Penny touching the wall to win at the exact same moment

Silver and Gold — Again

The Olympics weren't over for Simone. In the 50-meter freestyle, she earned a silver medal. In the 4 x 100 freestyle relay, she helped her team win another silver.

Simone had one more race — the 4 x 100 medley relay. Simone and teammates Kathleen Baker, Lilly King, and Dana Vollmer showed Team USA's true power. Kathleen swam first. She quickly took the lead. But then she fell behind. By the time Lilly dove in to replace her, Denmark, Canada, and Australia were ahead.

Swimming the breaststroke, Lilly pulled the United States back into first. Then Russia raced ahead. Lilly finished her leg. Dana dove in. She brought the United States back into the lead. At the wall, Simone was waiting.

Simone swam last. With a strong lead set by Dana, it was up to Simone to keep the team's lead. In her last lap, Simone was a full body length ahead of her challengers. The United States was the clear winner. It was another Olympic gold!

FACT

The gold medal the women's swim team won in the 4 x 100 medley relay had special meaning. It was the 1,000th Olympic gold ever earned at the Summer Games.

Simone, Kathleen, Dana, and Lilly with their gold medals

CHAPTER 5

Back Home Again

Simone returned home from
Rio to major fanfare in Houston.
City leaders and even the
marching band from her high
school came to celebrate.
Fans snapped pictures as
she walked through the airport.
Simone spoke with them and showed off
her Olympic medals. She also gave a quick
interview to the local news media.

With the Olympics behind her, Simone
was ready to return to normal life. She
couldn't wait to have some home-cooked
meals. She made one quick stop after
leaving the airport. It was a trip to get
some of her favorite donuts.

> I never thought I would reach this many people. Just to have their support means a lot. It really keeps me going and pushes me to hopefully swim a little faster as I continue my career.
>
> —Simone Manuel to reporters at the Houston Airport, August 17, 2016

Simone speaks to reporters in Houston about her Olympic victories.

Life after Gold

After her gold medal wins, Simone Manuel became a household name. The media and the public were interested in what she had to say. Simone used this as an opportunity. She spoke about issues that mattered to her. One topic she addressed was racial tensions in the United States. In 2016 protests erupted across the country after police fatally shot black men in several cities. "It means a lot, especially with what is going on in the world today, some of the issues of police brutality," Simone told reporters. "This win hopefully brings hope and change to some of the issues that are going on."

She also spoke about busting the stereotype that African Americans can't do well in swimming. She started working with USA Swimming's "Make a Splash." The program gives free and low-cost lessons to children.

> I didn't have that many people to look up to when I was younger so hopefully it inspires other African Americans to get involved in the sport.

—Simone Manuel, *Today* interview, August 15, 2016

Back to School

Just a few weeks after the Olympics, Simone was back at Stanford. Now a college student again, her schedule was packed. She focused on balancing schoolwork with several swim practices each week. She also did weight lifting and cardio exercises.

Back with her college team, Simone proved she was still a superstar. She helped the Stanford women's team win the NCAA Championship in March 2017. Simone broke records in the 50- and 100-yard freestyle.

When she can, Simone squeezes in a social life too. She relaxes by singing, dancing, shopping, and watching movies.

FACT

Simone Manuel wasn't the only Olympic swimmer on Stanford's team. Katie Ledecky and Lia Neal swam for Stanford also.

Visions of 2020

Simone's swimming career is far from over. In 2017 she won gold in the 100-meter freestyle at the World Aquatic Championships in Budapest, Hungary.

Simone at the 2017 World Aquatic Championships

She has her sights set on the 2020 Summer Olympics in Tokyo. Simone has more athletic goals to achieve.

Simone also has her eye on her future beyond swimming. She thinks she might one day like to have a career in marketing and advertising.

Simone has already achieved so much. She has busted stereotypes and broken records along the way. Doing what she loves, she's created a lasting legacy and a foundation for more success in the future.

Timeline

1996 ·· born in Houston, Texas

2000 ·· begins taking swim lessons

2004 ·· Maritza Correia is the first black female
        swimmer to make the U.S. Olympic team.

2010 ·· begins attending Fort Bend Austin High
        School, in Sugar Land, Texas

2011 ·· competes internationally for the first time

2013 ·· sets record for age group in the 50-meter
        freestyle at the World Championships

2014 ·· breaks a national record in the
        50-meter freestyle

     ·· graduates high school and begins college
        at Stanford University

2016 ·· makes U.S. Olympic team

     ·· wins a historic Olympic gold medal; wins
        another gold with relay team and two
        silver medals

2017 ·· wins NCAA Championship with Stanford

     ·· wins gold in the 100-meter freestyle at the
        World Aquatics Championships

Read More

Lanser, Amanda. *The Science Behind Swimming, Diving, and Other Water Sports*. Science of the Summer Olympics. North Mankato, Minn.: Capstone Press, 2016.

Scheff, Matt. *Simone Manuel*. Olympic Stars. Minneapolis, Minn.: Abdo, 2017.

Smith, Nikkolas. *The Golden Girls of Rio*. New York: Sky Pony Press, 2016.

Internet Sites

Use FactHound to find Internet sites related to this book.

Visit *www.facthound.com*

Just type in 9781515797074 and go!

Check out projects, games and lots more at
www.capstonekids.com

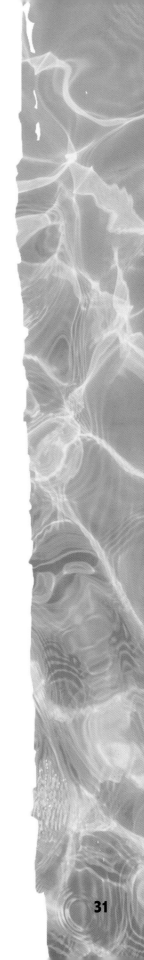

31

Index